ROES

CLEOPATRA

Calico Kid

An Imprint of Magic Wagon
abdobooks.com

by CHRISTINE PLATT
illustrated by ADDY RIVERA

Christine A. Platt is an author and scholar of African and African-American history. A beloved storyteller of the African diaspora, Christine enjoys writing historical fiction and non-fiction for people of all ages. You can learn more about her and her work at christineaplatt.com.

For every Queen. —CP

To those who work to make our world a better place. —AR

abdobooks.com

Published by Magic Wagon, a division of ABDO, PO Box 398166, Minneapolis, Minnesota 55439. Copyright © 2020 by Abdo Consulting Group, Inc. International copyrights reserved in all countries. No part of this book may be reproduced in any form without written permission from the publisher. Calico Kid™ is a trademark and logo of Magic Wagon.

Printed in the United States of America, North Mankato, Minnesota.
092019
012020

THIS BOOK CONTAINS
RECYCLED MATERIALS

Written by Christine Platt
Illustrated by Addy Rivera
Edited by Bridget O'Brien
Art Directed by Candice Keimig

Library of Congress Control Number: 2019942284

Publisher's Cataloging-in-Publication Data

Names: Platt, Christine, author. I Rivera, Addy, illustrator.
Title: Cleopatra / by Christine Platt ; illustrated by Addy Rivera.
Description: Minneapolis, Minnesota : Magic Wagon, 2020. I Series: Sheroes
Summary: This title introduces readers to Cleopatra and how she became a shero and one of the most famous female rulers of all time.
Identifiers: ISBN 9781532136412 (lib. bdg.) I ISBN 9781644943076 (pbk.) I ISBN 9781532137013 (ebook) I ISBN 9781532137310 (Read-to-Me ebook)
Subjects: LCSH: Cleopatra, Queen of Egypt, -30 B.C.–Juvenile literature. I Queens – Egypt – Biography–Juvenile literature. I Alexandria (Egypt)–History–Juvenile literature. I Ptolemies, Kings of Egypt–Juvenile literature. I Ptolemaic dynasty, 305-30 B.C.–Juvenile literature.
Classification: DDC 932.02 [B]–dc23

Table of Contents

CHAPTER #1
Girl with a Dream

Around 69 BCE, Pharaoh Ptolemy XII and Cleopatra V Tryphaena welcomed a daughter. Her name was Cleopatra VII Thea Philopator.

Pharaoh was the ruler of Egypt. His daughter would be the next leader. She would become one of the kingdom's most powerful rulers.

Cleopatra was Egypt's newest princess. But she wasn't Egyptian. She was from the Ptolemy dynasty. They were Greek.

For almost 300 years, every ruler of Egypt only spoke Greek. She would one day change this.

Cleopatra spent a lot of time with her father. She learned how to rule by watching him.

She had two brothers and a sister. But Cleopatra was her father's favorite child.

Cleopatra was wise beyond her years. She was helping her father rule by the time she was fourteen years old.

Egypt was successful and rich. She dreamed of making it even greater. She wanted it to become one of the most powerful kingdoms in the world.

CHAPTER #2

Woman on a Mission

Cleopatra helped her father rule until she was eighteen years old. When her father died, he left the throne to his oldest children.

It was common at the time for the siblings to marry. This was not for love. It made sure the family stayed in power.

Cleopatra was older than Ptolemy XIII. She served as the main ruler for several years.

But as her brother grew up, he wanted more power. This led to a family fight. He banned his sister so he could rule alone.

Cleopatra was mad. She planned to take back the throne. In 48 BCE, she saw her chance.

Julius Caesar was a Roman general. He was at odds with Cleopatra's brother.

She learned the general would be visiting the Egyptian city, Alexandria. She snuck into his living quarters.

Some historians say she hid in a sack. Others say she was wrapped inside carpet. But her disguise worked!

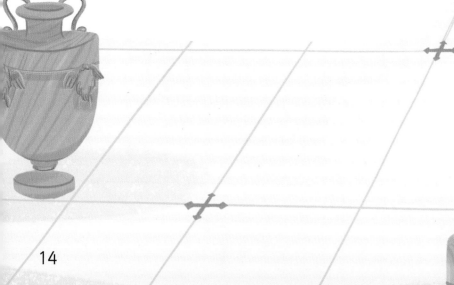

The general agreed to help the beautiful and wise former queen. In time, they fell in love.

They returned to Egypt. She challenged her brother to the throne. He was defeated during their civil war. He drowned in the Nile River.

Her other siblings died mysteriously. Many believe she had a hand in their deaths. This made sure they would not try to take the throne from her.

CHAPTER #3
So Smart, So Brave

Cleopatra successfully ruled her kingdom from a young age. She was also a good student. She studied many subjects. This included math, physics, art, medicine, and astronomy.

She learned how to speak several languages. They included Greek, Latin, and Hebrew.

She also did something even more surprising. She became the first ruler in her family to learn how to speak Egyptian.

Some people thought Cleopatra looked like the Egyptian goddess, Isis. Historians once believed that she used her looks to gain power.

But further discoveries have proven that wrong. Her beauty paled in comparison to her mind.

Plutarch, a famous Greek-Roman biographer, wrote about her cleverness and charm. He said they made people want to work with her.

Cleopatra was also brave. She
had a lot of power. Her life was in
constant danger, especially because
she was a woman. Her motives for
love were always questioned.

In 41 BCE, she began a relationship with Roman general, Mark Antony. The Roman Senate was mad.

But she truly loved him. She knew he would protect her. He would make sure she stayed in power.

The Roman Senate was still angry. They declared war on the couple in 32 BCE. This is known as the Battle of Actium.

But the couple fought for their love. Cleopatra even bravely led naval warships.

Unfortunately, they were defeated.
They fled to Egypt. Still, her bravery
in battle is thought of as a major
moment in history.

CHAPTER #4
A Real Shero

Cleopatra served as one of Egypt's most powerful leaders for almost thirty years. During this time, she had four children.

Her first child was Caesarion. His father is believed to be Julius Caesar.

She had three children with Mark Antony. This included twins, Alexander Helios and Cleopatra Selene. Their youngest was Ptolemy Philadelphus.

Cleopatra died on August 12, 30 BCE. Mark Antony heard a false rumor that she had been killed. He took his own life. Upon learning of Mark Antony's death, historians believe she did the same.

The two were buried side by side. Over time, historians have searched for their graves. But they have never been found.

Cleopatra was the last true Pharaoh of Egypt. Her life has captivated people for a long time. From literary works to theater productions, the world continues to honor her.

Cleopatra inspired William Shakespeare's well-known play, *Antony and Cleopatra.* The Hollywood movie, *Cleopatra,* and several books were also based on her life.

Even to this day, Cleopatra is a true shero. She remains one of the most famous female rulers of all time.

Booklinks
NONFICTION NETWORK
FREE! ONLINE NONFICTION RESOURCES

To learn more about *Cleopatra*, please visit abdobooklinks.com or scan this QR code. These links are routinely monitored and updated to provide the most current information available.